THE GREAT PHILOSOPHERS

Consulting Editors
Ray Monk and Frederic Raphael

KANT

Ralph Walker

ROUTLEDGE
New York

Published in 1999 by
Routledge
29 West 35th Street
New York, NY 10001

First published in 1997 by
Phoenix
A Division of the Orion Publishing Group Ltd.
Orion House
5 Upper Saint Martin's Lane
London WC2H 9EA

10 9 8 7 6 5 4 3 2 1

Library of Congress Cataloging-in-Publication Data

Walker, Ralph Charles Sutherland.
        Kant / Ralph Walker.
         p. cm.—(The great philosophers : 13)
        Includes bibliographical references.
        ISBN 0-415-92388-3 (pbk.)
        1. Kant, Immanuel, 1724–1804—Ethics. 2. Ethics.
        I. Title. II. Series:Great Philosophers (Routledge
        (Firm)) : 13.
B2799.E8W27 1999
170'.92—dc21   99-21669
                                                    CIP

KANT

and the moral law

INTRODUCTORY NOTE

Any account of Kant's ideas must involve interpretation. At some points my interpretation is inevitably controversial; some different views may be found in the Further Reading listed at the end. For help in clarifying my own thoughts I am grateful to many people, particularly my pupils, and especially Angus Ritchie.

The standard edition of Kant's work is the one published by the Deutsche Akademie der Wissenschaften as *Kant's gesammelte Schriften* (Berlin, 1900–), often abbreviated 'Ak'. English translations of Kant's works usually carry its page references in their margins. In what follows, references are to this edition, except in two cases. Following convention, references to the *Critique of Pure Reason* are to the pages of the first and second editions; and references to Kant's private notes (*Reflexionen*) are by note number as set out in the Akademie edition.

References to Kant's works are abbreviated as follows. Where they are to the Akademie edition, the relevant volume is shown.

A/B   First (1781)/second (1787) edition of the *Critique of Pure Reason*.

G   *Groundwork of the Metaphysics of Morals* (1785; Ak. IV)

M   *Metaphysics of Morals* (1797; Ak. VI)

P   *Critique of Practical Reason* (1788; Ak. V)

Pr   *Prolegomena to any Future Metaphysics* (1783; Ak. IV)

3

R   *Religion Within the Limits of Reason Alone* (1793; Ak. VI)

Rf   *Reflexionen* (Ak. XIX)

The translations I have used are my own, but authoritative translations of Kant's works are appearing in the Cambridge Edition of the Works of Immanuel Kant (Cambridge University Press, Cambridge, 1993–); the volume entitled *Practical Philosophy* is particularly good, and contains translations by Mary Gregor of most of Kant's moral works. There are also excellent translations of the *Groundwork* by H. J. Paton, under the title *The Moral Law* (Hutchinson, London, 3rd edn, 1956), and by L. W. Beck, under the title *Foundations of the Metaphysics of Morals* (Liberal Arts, New York, 1959). Beck's translation is included with his translations of other works of Kant's in his *Kant's Critique of Practical Reason and Other Writings in Moral Philosophy* (University of Chicago Press, Chicago, 1949).

The best translation of the *Critique of Pure Reason* currently available is the one by Norman Kemp Smith (Macmillan, London, 1929).

THE MORAL LAW

Kant holds there is an objective moral law. It is known to us not from experience, but by reason. It binds us to act, or to abstain from acting, simply on the grounds that the action is required by the law or forbidden by it. It is a 'categorical imperative': neither its authority, nor its power to motivate us, is derived from anything but itself.

Then as now, most philosophers viewed morality very differently. Some thought there was an objective moral law, but that it depended on God's will. Others thought morality was to do with reason, but that the reasoning was all about how to promote some objective, like one's own happiness or the welfare of society. These ideas Kant rejected, because they make morality depend on something outside itself: God's will, or the desire to promote welfare. He rejected equally the idea that morality is the natural development of certain feelings which belong to our human nature, and nothing more. That would not be compatible with its inherently rational character.

Let us add that unless you want to deny to the concept of morality all truth, and any relationship between it and any possible object, you cannot deny that its law is of such broad significance that it holds not only for human beings, but for all *rational beings in general*; and not just under contingent conditions and with exceptions, but *absolutely necessarily*. It is clear that no experience could give us occasion to infer even the possibility of such apodeictic [i.e. necessary] laws. For by what right can we make something an object of unlimited respect, as a universal prescription for every rational nature, if it may perhaps only be valid under the contingent conditions of humanity? And why should laws of the determination of *our* will be held to be laws of the determination of the will of a rational being in general – and only as such laws for our will too – if these laws were merely empirical, instead of having their origin entirely *a priori* in pure, yet practical, reason? (G 408)

By '*a priori*' Kant means 'independent of experience': knowledge is *a priori* if it is 'independent of experience and even of all impressions of the senses' (B 2). The truths known by pure reason are *a priori*. They include logical laws, and certain other truths about the world set out in *The Critique of Pure Reason*. They include also the moral law. Truths knowable only by experience are called *a posteriori*.

The law claims obedience in its own right. I would have a *moral* reason to obey God's commands only if I knew he had issued the right commands.

Even the Holy One of the Gospel must first be compared with our ideal of moral perfection, before one can recognize him as such; indeed he says of himself: Why do you call me (whom you see) good? No one is good (the archetype of the good) except only God (whom you do not see). But from where do we have the concept of God as the highest good? Simply from the *idea* of moral perfection which reason draws up *a priori*. (G 408–9)

Likewise morality cannot depend on our desires. It does not derive its value from its usefulness in promoting happiness, or any other objective we find attractive. It has

6

its value in itself, and if happiness has a *value* – as opposed to just being something we seek – it can get it only *from* the moral law, which is the source of moral value. The moral law does not, therefore, get its binding force from its ability to promote some objective of ours. It just tells us what we ought to do. This is what Kant means by calling it 'categorical'.

> All *imperatives* command either *hypothetically* or *categorically* ... If the action [commanded] would be good simply as a means *to something else*, then the imperative is *hypothetical*; but if the action is represented as good *in itself*, and thus as a necessary principle for a will which is in itself in accordance with reason, then the imperative is *categorical*. (G 414)

By 'imperatives' Kant does not just mean 'commands': he means 'commands of reason'. An imperative is 'a rule which is indicated by an "ought" ... and which signifies that, if reason completely determined the will, the action would infallibly take place in accordance with this rule' (P 20).

Many people think an action can be rational only as the rational means to some desired end. They agree there are hypothetical imperatives, but deny that any action can be rational in its own right, independently of its tendency to fulfil the agent's goals. Thus Hume thought reason could only be 'the slave of the passions'.[1] Our 'passions', our desires and preferences, determine our objectives, and reason only works out how to achieve them. Kant thinks reason prescribes categorical imperatives as well. Certain actions are obligatory just because reason demands them.

The difference between categorical and hypothetical imperatives does not lie in whether they are expressed by using an 'if'. The categorical imperatives of morality are often very sensitive to the details of particular cases, as Kant was well aware. They can therefore often best be formulated 'If you are in circumstances X, you ought to do Y'. The contrast is rather that a hypothetical imperative says that an action is rational as the means of achieving some objective; nothing is implied about the rationality of having that objective. A categorical imperative tells us what is rational in its own right, and therefore, according to Kant, moral.

This may suggest Kant sees morality as a matter of rigid rules. He has often been interpreted in that way, but wrongly. The interpretation derives mainly from his *Groundwork of the Metaphysics of Morals*, but that was written as a popular book, in which Kant attempted simplifications that gave rise to misunderstandings. Other works, particularly *The Metaphysics of Morals*, make it clear that the moral law is *not* a set of rigid rules. He repeatedly shows himself sensitive to the complexities of difficult cases, and raises a series of 'casuistical questions' – questions about concrete moral issues, where he does not think the answers are at all obvious. They cannot be resolved by any simple appeal to rules. (He uses 'casuistical' in its proper sense – to do with the moral assessment of specific cases; it carries no pejorative overtone.) Kant talks about 'the moral *law*' to stress the imperative character of morality; he does not mean it can be neatly codified.

Moreover, it is explained in the *Metaphysics of Morals* that morality is largely concerned with promoting certain ends. To that extent again rules are out of place, for

it leaves room (*latitudo*) in the following (observance) of the law for free choice; that is, the law cannot precisely

lay down how one is to act and how much one is to do
in furthering the end that is also a duty. (M 390)

These ideas are present in the *Groundwork*, but so obscurely
that they are easily missed. He does say that every 'maxim',
or subjective principle on which one can act, must lay
down some end (G 436). He also says that to act morally is
to act from a maxim which lays it down that we must treat
rational beings, and human beings in particular, as ends;
'ends in themselves'.

> Now I say that man, and in general every rational being,
> *exists* as end in itself, *not merely as means* to be used by
> this or that will as it pleases. Such a being must, in all his
> actions, whether they are directed to himself or to other
> rational beings as well, always be regarded *at the same
> time as an end.* (G 428)

The categorical imperative can therefore be formulated: 'So
act that you treat humanity, both in your own person and
in the person of every other human being, never merely as
a means, but always at the same time as an end' (G 429).
But the *Groundwork* leaves it unclear what this means.
Evidently Kant thinks we should treat one another with
some sort of equality of respect, but that is rather vague,
and it is not explained how people can be called 'ends' at
all. Ends are objectives, things we can aim to achieve.

In the *Metaphysics of Morals* he explains that there are
certain 'ends that are also duties'.

> **Which are the ends that are also duties?**
> They are: *one's own perfection* and *the happiness of
> others.*
>
> These cannot be interchanged to make *one's own*

happiness and *the perfection of others* into ends which would be, in themselves, duties for the same person.

For *one's own happiness* is an end that indeed all human beings have (thanks to the impulses of their nature). But this end can never be regarded as a duty, without contradicting oneself. What everyone already wants unavoidably, of his own accord, does not belong under the concept of *duty*; for duty is a *necessitation* to an unwillingly adopted end. So it would be contradictory to say: one *has a duty* to further one's own happiness with all one's powers.

Similarly this is a contradiction: to make another's *perfection* my end and to hold myself duty-bound to advance it. For the *perfection* of another human being, as a person, consists in this, that he *himself* is able to set himself his end in accordance with his own concepts of duty. And it would be contradictory to require (i.e. to make it my duty) that I should do something that nobody except the other himself can do. (M 385–6)

The duty to seek my own perfection is the duty to develop my capacities, particularly moral and intellectual capacities, but physical ones too, since without them I cannot act effectively. The duty to seek others' happiness is the duty to promote their objectives; the satisfaction of their desires and of their individual projects.

When it comes to happiness, the promotion of which as an end is my duty, it must be the happiness of *other* people, *whose* (permitted) *end I hereby also* make *my own*. What they may count as belonging to their happiness remains up to themselves to decide; though it is also up to me to refuse many things *they* think will make them happy, if I disagree with them about that, provided these are not things they have a right to demand of me as their own. (M 388)

The bracketed word 'permitted' is important. Someone might have an end that conflicted with the duty to further his own perfection or others' happiness, and that could not be a permitted end. Moreover, people often have objectives that interfere with or exploit other people. The basic principle of what Kant calls the Doctrine of Right is that it is wrong to interfere with the freedom of others, a freedom they need for their own self-development.

Universal Principle of Right

'Every action is *right* if it or its maxim allows each person's freedom of choice to coexist with the freedom of everyone in accordance with a universal law.'

Thus if my action, or in general my situation, can coexist with the freedom of everyone in accordance with a universal law, anyone who hinders me in these respects does me wrong; for this hindrance (this resistance) cannot coexist with freedom in accordance with universal laws. (M 230–1)

As this suggests, Kant recognizes that an action can be morally indifferent – neither obligatory nor forbidden. People often think he did not recognize this, but he did.

An action is *permitted* (*licitum*) if it is not contrary to obligation; and this freedom which is unlimited by any contrary imperative is called *being authorized* (*facultas moralis*). From this it is self-evident what is meant by *not permitted* (*illicitum*). (M 222)

An action that is neither required nor forbidden is merely *permitted*, because in relation to it there is no law to limit freedom (i.e., to limit one's being authorized) and thus also no duty. Such an action is called morally indifferent. (M 223)

The true strength of virtue is a *quiet mind* with a reflective and firm determination to put its law into practice. That is the condition of *health* in the moral life ... But someone is called 'fancifully virtuous' if he recognizes none of the *things which are indifferent* (*adiaphora*) in relation to morality, and strews all his steps with duties, as with mantraps. He does not find it indifferent whether I nourish myself with meat or fish, or with beer or wine, if both agree with me. 'Fanciful virtue' is a concern with tiny details which would turn virtue's dominion into tyranny if it were adopted into the doctrine of virtue. (M 409)

But now: if Kant thinks the moral law requires us to promote happiness, is he not a utilitarian?

Utilitarians think the moral value of an act depends on its consequences: whether it increases happiness. The act gets its value from the consequences. For Kant the moral value of an act depends on the moral law, not on any consequences. The difference is subtle but important. For the utilitarian, happiness obviously has value, and morality is concerned with how to get there. Kant would say that the utilitarian's imperatives were only hypothetical, telling us how to achieve an assumed goal. On his own view, it is the moral law itself that requires us to pursue those ends that are also duties, and their value is derived entirely from the law, which lays them down as obligatory. What matters is that the idea of these ends 'arises out of morality and is not the foundation of morality' (R 5). The only source of value is the moral law, and so the only intrinsically valuable thing is a will guided by that law.

> It is impossible to conceive of anything in the world, or even out of it, that can be considered good without qualification, except a **good will**. (G 393)

> A good will is not good because of what it effects or accomplishes, nor through its fitness for attaining some proposed end, but only through its willing; that is, it is good in itself. Considered in itself, it is to be valued incomparably more highly than anything it could ever bring about to satisfy some inclination, or even (if you like) the sum total of all inclinations. Even if, through some special disfavour of destiny, or through the grudging endowment of step-motherly nature, this will wholly lacked the power to carry through its intentions; even if by its utmost effort it still accomplished nothing, and only the good will was left (not of course as a mere wish, but as the calling up of every means in our power); even then it would shine forth in its own right as a jewel, as something which has its full value in itself. (G 394)

This is not to deny that happiness has a value, but its value is given to it by the law. In fact Kant thinks that the 'highest good' consists in an overall unity of virtue and happiness.

> That *virtue* (as worthiness to be happy) is the *supreme condition* of everything that can even seem to us worth wanting, and thus of all our claims to happiness, and is thus the *supreme* good, has been proved ... But this does not make it the complete and perfect good, the object of the desiring faculty of rational finite beings. For that *happiness* is also required ... Now if virtue and

happiness together constitute possession of the highest good in a single person, so likewise happiness, distributed exactly in proportion to morality – as the worth of the person and his worthiness to be happy – constitutes the *highest good* of a possible world; and that means the complete and perfect good. Within it virtue is always the supreme good, being a condition that has no further condition above it; whereas happiness is something always pleasant to its possessor, yet not good for itself alone absolutely and in every respect, but instead always presupposing conduct in accordance with the moral law as its condition. (P 110–11)

Still,

though the highest good may be the whole *object* of a pure practical reason, that is, of a pure will, it must not therefore be taken to be its *determining ground*. The moral law alone must be seen as the ground for making the highest good and its production or promotion to be the object. (P 109)

All moral value derives from the law.

DUTY

Why did Kant think of morality in this way? In the *Groundwork* he explains that his method is to start with what people actually think, with the 'ordinary rational knowledge of morality'. The aim is not just to describe people's beliefs (which are often rather confused), but to analyse them so as to reveal our underlying conception of morality. This is what he means by saying that in the first two chapters he proceeds 'analytically':

> In this book I have adopted the method I have because I believe it is best if one first proceeds analytically from ordinary knowledge to the determination of its supreme principle, and then back again synthetically from the examination of this principle and its sources to the ordinary knowledge in which we find it used. (G 392)

It is one thing to show that a certain conception of morality underlies ordinary thought, and another to show that it is true.[2] Kant is well aware of this. At the end of the second chapter he says

> By developing the concept of morality that is universally current, we have only shown that autonomy of the will is unavoidably connected with it – or rather lies at its foundation. So anyone who takes morality to be something real, and not a chimerical idea lacking truth, must admit the principle of morality that has been brought forward. This chapter, therefore, like the first, has been merely analytic. That morality is not a phantom of the

15

> brain … can be shown only by a *possible synthetic use of pure practical reason.* (G 445)

The third chapter is supposed to vindicate morality by arguing 'synthetically'.[3] He explains that when he argued synthetically he went about things 'in such a way that I investigated within pure reason itself, and sought to determine in this source itself, in accordance with principles, the elements and the laws of its pure employment' (Pr 274). Later we shall see how far he succeeds in vindicating morality.

The first chapter of the *Groundwork* develops the thought that morality, as we ordinarily conceive it, is – to use a modern term – prescriptive. To say morality is prescriptive is to say that one cannot be aware of a moral requirement without recognizing it as a reason for acting (if the circumstances allow it to be acted on). Moral requirements differ in this respect from hypothetical imperatives. I can recognize that the best way to save money is to invest it with Midas & Midas, without seeing that as a reason for acting, since I may not want to save money. I can recognize that the best way to secure happiness is by keeping fit, without seeing that as a reason for acting, since there is nothing to *require* me to want happiness. But moral requirements are automatically reasons for action: they are categorical imperatives.

I may have a reason for acting, and yet not act. I can choose freely whether to do what morality requires. But I cannot choose to ignore the fact that the moral law gives me a reason for acting. It is there as a motive for me to act on, even if it is not the motive on which I choose to act. Being intrinsically prescriptive, morality can be called a law; which does not mean it can be reduced to a neat set of rules. It guides conduct and provides reasons for action. That is why it must be the source of value.

He sets out three 'propositions' that take this idea further. The first is initially puzzling. It can be summarized: 'The only thing that can give an action moral worth is its being done out of a sense of duty.' If one performs an action just because one wants to, it has no moral worth.

> To do good to others, where one can, is a duty; besides this, there are many people of so sympathetic a nature that – even without any other motive of vanity or self-interest – they find an inner pleasure in spreading joy around them, and can be delighted at the contentment of others so far as they have brought it about. But I maintain that in such a case an action of this kind, however much it may be in accordance with duty, and however amiable it may be, still has no true moral worth. It stands on the same footing as other inclinations, like the inclination to seek honour, which, when it fortunately leads to something which is in fact in the common interest, and in accordance with duty, and consequently honourable, deserves praise and encouragement, but never esteem. For its maxim lacks moral content, namely that of doing such actions not out of inclination but *out of duty*. Suppose, then, that the mind of this philanthrophist were overclouded by his own sorrow, which extinguished all sympathy for the fate of others, but that he still had the power to do good to others in distress, though other people's distress no longer moved him, because he was sufficiently preoccupied with his own. Suppose also that now, when no longer moved to it by any inclination, he tears himself out of this deadly insensibility and performs the action

without any inclination, simply out of duty. Now for the first time his action has its genuine moral worth. Still further: if nature had placed little sympathy in the heart of this or that person; and if he (otherwise a decent man) were by temperament cold and indifferent to the sufferings of others, perhaps because he was himself provided with the special gift of patience and endurance towards his own sufferings, and expected or demanded the same of others; if nature had not exactly designed such a man to be a philanthropist (though in truth he would not be her worst product), would he not find in himself a source from which he might give himself a far higher worth than that which a good-natured temperament may have? Certainly! It is just here that there begins that worth of character that is moral and incomparably the highest: that he does good, not out of inclination, but out of duty. (G 398–9)

Two comments are needed. First, the action of someone who enjoys kindness is entirely *right*. Kant distinguishes between actions 'in accordance with duty' and actions done 'out of duty'. Only the latter reflect credit on the agent. But actions in accordance with duty do not transgress the moral law, even though they are not done for the sake of it. They are not wrong actions; they are the right thing to do, but done for the wrong reasons. To say they 'lack moral worth' is just to say they reflect no credit on the agent. They are 'right' but not 'virtuous'.

Moreover, Kant is not denying that someone who enjoys acting kindly *may* do so from a sense of duty. The person whose action lacks moral worth is motivated *only* by inclination and *not* by duty. He is lucky to have socially desirable inclinations, but he is acting on inclination as much as someone who exploits others for his own gain. The person who spreads happiness out of a sense of duty does so because he knows this is what the moral law requires. And Kant does not think that only people of cold and indifferent temperament can act out of duty. His point is that in them action out of duty would be easier to detect. But a properly virtuous person will be one in whom there is a 'firmly grounded disposition to fulfill one's duty exactly' (R 23n), and such a person will certainly enjoy dutiful action.

> Now if one asks, 'What is the *aesthetic* character, or the *temperament of virtue*? Is it courageous, and so *joyful*, or is it fear-ridden and cast down?', an answer is hardly necessary. The latter slavish frame of mind can never exist without a hidden *hatred* of the law, and a heart which is joyful in *following* its duty (not just contented in recognizing it) is a sign of the genuineness of the virtuous disposition (R 23–4n)

In these contexts 'aesthetic' means for Kant 'related to pleasure'.

One might still think Kant's dutiful person will be unattractively austere, enjoying duty but never acting from love, or sympathy, or any warm human emotion. That again would be wrong. The moral law *can* motivate me to action directly, but it can also function as a second-order motive, enabling me to decide which of my emotions to act on and to what extent. We are free agents, not driven mechanically by our passions, and so we need some way of deciding which of them to act on; the moral law provides such a way.

> Freedom of the will is of a quite special character, in that

no incentive can determine it to any action, *except insofar as the agent has incorporated it in his maxim* (has made it a universal rule in accordance with which he will conduct himself); only in this way can an incentive, whatever it may be, coexist with the absolute spontaneity of the will (i.e. of freedom). (R 23–4)

Kant actually holds that the cultivation of feelings like sympathy is itself a duty. They serve a dual purpose. They enable us, naturally and easily, to do what is right much of the time; they are 'indeed helpful to the good will itself and can make its work very much easier' (G 393). They also help us to understand other people, and give us the sensitivity needed for decisions in difficult cases.

Although it is not in itself a duty to share the joys and sufferings of others, an active sympathy for their fate is a duty. It is at least an indirect duty for the purpose of cultivating sympathetic natural (aesthetic) feelings in ourselves, and using these as so many means to a sympathy based on moral principles and on the feeling appropriate to them. (M 457)

What *would* be wrong would be to let oneself be carried away by one's feelings, sympathetic or otherwise. One must always be guided by the sense of duty.

His second proposition is:

an action out of duty has its moral worth *not in the purpose* which is to be achieved by it, but in the maxim in accordance with which it is decided on. It depends therefore not on the realization of the object of the action, but merely on the *principle of volition*, in accordance with which the action has taken place without regard to any objects of the faculty of desire. (G 399–400)

What gives an action moral worth is the 'maxim', the subjective principle, on which the agent acts; the agent's maxim will have to be something like 'I shall do whatever the law requires, which in this situation is XYZ.' In saying it is not the purpose that matters, he means that the action does not derive its worth from its being aimed at some goal, like happiness, which has value independently of the law.

He emphasizes the third proposition: *'Duty is the necessity of acting out of respect for the law'* (G 400). 'Necessity' is used technically here. It does not mean that to act out of duty is to act automatically, without free will; quite the contrary. Kant contrasts our situation with that of a 'holy will', like God. The idea of duty applies only to beings like ourselves, who can be deflected from duty by other desires, and for whom duty appears as a kind of necessitation – in fact, as an 'ought'. It does not apply to a holy will.

'Respect' (*Achtung* – sometimes translated 'reverence') is Kant's word for the moral motive. Respect differs from our non-moral inclinations:

For an object as the effect of my proposed action I can indeed have an *inclination*, but *never respect*, just because it is merely an effect and not the activity of a will. Similarly I cannot have respect for inclination as such, whether it be mine or that of another; in the first case I can at most approve it, in the second case I can sometimes even love it, that is, regard it as to my own advantage. The only thing that can be an object of respect, and thus a command, is something that is connected with my will simply as ground, never as effect; something that does not serve my inclination, but

21

outweighs it, or at least excludes it altogether from the calculations involved in making a choice; in other words, the law in its own right. Now an action out of duty must set aside entirely the influence of inclination, and with it every object of the will. So nothing remains which can determine the will except objectively the *law* and subjectively *pure respect* for this practical law, and thus the maxim of obeying such a law, even at the expense of all my inclinations. (G 400)

This leaves it obscure what exactly respect is, and it is not much clarified by his attempt to explain himself.

It might be objected that behind the word 'respect' I have only sought refuge in an obscure feeling, instead of giving a clear answer to the question through a concept of reason. But although respect is indeed a feeling, it is not one *received* through outside influence, but a feeling *self-produced* by a rational concept and therefore different in kind from all feelings of the first variety, which can be reduced to fear or inclination. What I recognize immediately as law for me, I recognize with respect, which means simply the consciousness of the *subordination* of my will to a law without the mediation of other influences on my senses. The immediate determination of the will by the law and the consciousness of this determination is called *respect*, so that respect is regarded as the *effect* of the law on the subject and not as the *cause* of the law. Respect is properly the representation of a value which destroys my self-love. (G 401n)

So is it really a special kind of feeling, or just a rational awareness of the moral law? Kant seems ambivalent. Later in the *Groundwork* he appears to come down in favour of the idea that 'interest' is needed, over and above awareness of the moral law, if we are to be motivated to action. He admits it is mysterious how interest relates to the law.

> An interest is that by which reason becomes practical, that is, that by which it becomes a cause determining the will. (G 459n)

> In order to will that which reason alone prescribes to a rational being affected by the senses in the form of an 'ought', it is certainly required that reason have the power to *infuse* a *feeling of pleasure* or of well-being at the fulfilment of a duty, and so there is required a causality of reason, by which it can determine the sensibility in accordance with its principles. But it is wholly impossible to understand, that is, to render comprehensible *a priori*, how a mere thought, which contains nothing that has to do with sensibility, can produce a feeling of pleasure or displeasure ... Thus for us human beings it is entirely impossible to explain how and why *the universality of the maxim as a law*, and therefore morality, should interest us. (G 460)

He got clearer, though, as time went on. It is simply my rational awareness of the objective law that motivates me. There is no reason to assimilate it to a feeling, which is something quite different and non-rational. So

> there is in the subject in *advance* of action no feeling determined towards morality. That is impossible, for all feelings are sensible, whereas the incentive of the moral disposition must be free of every sensible condiction ... And thus respect for the law is not the incentive to morality, but rather it is morality itself, subjectively

considered as an incentive; for by destroying all the claims of self-love which are in opposition to it, pure practical reason brings about esteem for the law, which now alone has influence. (P 75–6)

Kant's difficulties are due to the fact that his idea is both new and important. A law that is entirely objective – independent of the 'contingent conditions of humanity' (G 408), and in its own right binding on all rational beings in general – can motivate us to act simply through our awareness of it; and no rational being can be aware of it without recognizing it as a reason for action. It is thus objective in a very strong sense, holding quite independently of what anyone thinks or feels about it, but it is also prescriptive.

Is this coherent? Some would say not, though they offer little argument.[4] Kant's answer is that the moral law has essentially the same status as the principles of theoretical inference. These too are objective and prescriptive. They guide us not in action but in argument, but otherwise the parallel holds: nobody could recognize a principle like 'if P, and if P then Q, then Q', without seeing that it constituted a *reason* for inferring 'Q', given the truth of the premises.

But how is consciousness of the moral law possible? We can become conscious of pure practical laws in the same way that we are conscious of pure theoretical principles, by attending to the necessity with which reason prescribes them, and the setting aside of all empirical conditions which reason directs. (P 30)

Some people would object that action and argument are too different to allow us to speak of reason as 'prescribing' in the same sense in the two cases. One can know what one

24

ought to do and yet fail to do it; can one see that one's premises entail a conclusion, and yet refuse to draw it? This is debatable, but perhaps one can. It would certainly be irrational, but self-deception often seems to work like this: one refuses to draw a conclusion (e.g., that one's child is dead) though one can see it follows from true premises.

Others would deny that either kind of principle can be *objectively* binding on us: objectively, that is, in the sense Kant wants. Theoretical principles, they would say, are only habits of human thought, deriving from our psychology and 'the contingent conditions of humanity'. Hume held this, just as he held that our moral principles are the natural development of attitudes that belong to human nature. Others have held it since, notably Quine, who regards these features of human psychology as the natural result of evolution.[5] It amounts to a rejection of the *a priori* altogether.

> Nothing worse could happen to these efforts [of mine] than that someone should make the unexpected discovery that there neither was, nor could be, any *a priori* knowledge at all. But there is no danger of this. It would amount to someone's wanting to prove through reason that there is no such thing as reason. For we only say that we know something through reason when we are conscious that we could have known it even if it had not thus presented itself to us in experience; so that rational knowledge and knowledge *a priori* are one and the same. To seek to squeeze necessity out of an empirical proposition, 'as water out of pumice stone', and to seek to provide a judgement with the true universality that goes with necessity (and without which there is no rational inference, and therefore no inference by anal-

25

ogy, since analogy at least presumes universality and objective necessity and thus always presupposes these) – this would be a complete contradiction. To substitute subjective necessity, i.e. custom, for objective necessity, which is only to be found in *a priori* judgements, amounts to denying that reason has the power to judge about an object, i.e. to know it and to know what is true of it. It amounts to denying for example that, when something has happened frequently, and always after a particular preceding circumstance, we can *infer* from the one to the other (for this would require objective necessity and the concept of an *a priori* connection). Instead we could only wait for similar cases, in the same way as animals do. That would be to reject the concept of cause as fundamentally fallacious and as a mere delusion of thought. (P 12)

Hume had mounted just such an attack on the concept of cause, and had found no basis but custom or habit for our inductive expectation that past regularities will continue into the future. Kant's objection is that without such *a priori* principles we can know nothing: to gain knowledge from experience we must *interpret* experience, and we can interpret experience only if we have principles to interpret it with – principles that experience cannot itself supply. This objection constitutes the basis of his full-scale answer to Hume, developed in the *Critique of Pure Reason*, where he defends both the inductive principle and the concept of cause as indispensable for any knowledge at all. In the present context he thinks he need not insist on the point, for he believes that even Hume admitted we have *some a priori* knowledge.

Hume would be quite happy with this *system of*

universal empiricism in principles ... But not even Hume made his empiricism so universal as to include mathematics in it ... If one took the empiricism of principles *universally*, even mathematics would be included. (P 13)

So radical a denial of the *a priori*, Kant thinks, would be absurd.

In this philosophical and critical age it is difficult to take this empiricism seriously, and it is presumably put forward only as an exercise for judgement and in order to set in a clearer light, through the contrast, the necessity that belongs to rational *a priori* principles. One can therefore be grateful to those who want to trouble themselves with this otherwise uninstructive task. (P 14)

Actually he was wrong about Hume. Hume did want to reject the *a priori* altogether.[6] Quine, too, denies *a priori* status even to elementary logical principles. Against this Kant says that such philosophers rely on rational principles themselves, and could not argue unless they accepted them as valid. He could also have used his argument that without *a priori* principles no knowledge or experience would be possible. And if even one theoretical principle has to be admitted as both objective and prescriptive, there can be no force in the objection that objective prescriptions are impossible.

That would not establish that moral principles *are* objectively binding. Here Kant is seeking to show only that this is the conception of morality underlying ordinary thought. The *Groundwork*'s first chapter ends by saying that the analysis of this conception needs to be taken further. Before that, though, he introduces a further point: the law must be a *universal* law.

But what kind of law can it be, the representation of which must determine the will even without regard to the results expected from it, if this will is to be called absolutely and without qualification good? Since I have robbed the will of every impulsion that could arise for it as a consequence of following any law, there remains nothing that can serve the will as its principle except the universal conformity to law of actions in general. That is to say, I ought never to act except in such a way *that I could also will that my maxim should become a universal law.* Here it is the mere conformity to law in general (without basing it on any particular law for specific actions) that serves the will as its principle, and has to do so if duty is not to be everywhere an empty delusion and a chimerical concept. Ordinary human reason agrees completely with this in its practical judgements, and has this principle constantly before its eyes. (G 402)

We shall return to the question why it must be universal. But Kant is *not* here saying that there can be nothing to the law except the bare form of universality. He is saying only that the will must obey the universal law for its own sake, not for the sake of any outcome or payoff, or anything that is specific to a particular case and intrinsically non-universal.

One final question arises about duty. What about someone who, out of a misguided sense of duty, performs profoundly wicked acts? Will Kant not have to say that his actions have moral worth? No.

Take for example an inquisitor, who adheres firmly to the exclusiveness of his statutory faith to the point of martyring people, and who has to judge a so-called heretic (who is otherwise a good citizen) accused of unbelief. Now I ask whether, if he condemns him to death, one could say that he has followed his (no doubt erroneous) conscience, or whether one could not rather accuse him of a complete *lack of conscience*, whether he just erred or consciously did wrong. (R 186)

For to act from conscience – to act out of a sense of duty – is to act as pure practical reason requires; in other words, to obey the moral law. 'Conscience is practical reason holding a person's duty before him for his acquittal or condemnation in every case that comes under a law' (M 400). The inquisitor does not listen to the voice of practical reason. He has confused his own feelings with the rational demands of morality. This is easy to do, as Kant says at the end of the first chapter of the *Groundwork*. But it is a fundamental moral failing; one that can be cured only by reflection and by listening for the voice of reason.

THE CATEGORICAL IMPERATIVE

The second chapter of the *Groundwork* carries the analysis further, but whereas before the emphasis was on the prescriptiveness of the moral law, now the emphasis is on its rationality. To say that the moral law is rational, or known by pure practical reason, is to say that it is known *a priori*. It cannot be learnt from experience, and Kant claims that Hume's account of morality, as only the product of natural human attitudes, is inconsistent with our ordinary view: 'you cannot deny that its law is of such broad significance that it holds not only for human beings, but for *all rational beings in general*' (G 408). That is plausible; people normally do think the foundations of morality would be shaken if Hume could be shown to be right.

After introducing the moral law as a categorical imperative, he again seems to imply that it must be formal and empty.

> But if I think of a *categorical* imperative I know immediately what it contains. For since the imperative contains nothing besides the law, and the necessity that the maxim should conform to this law; and since the law contains no condition to limit it; there remains nothing but the universality of a law in general to which the maxim of the action should conform, and it is this conformity alone that the imperative properly presents as necessary.
>
> There is therefore only a single categorical imperative and it is this: *act only on that maxim through which you*

can at the same time will that it should become a universal law. (G 420–1)

This is misleading. By oversimplifying, Kant creates needless problems for the reader. He is not saying that the law has no content. It 'contains no condition to limit it' because it is not subordinate to some goal, in the way a hypothetical imperative is. With the categorical imperative all that is required is that the maxim must conform to the law. Now Kant thinks that the law must be universal, and that it must have something important to do with *willing*. Neither of these points is immediately obvious, though it is convenient to him to gloss that over. They both require comment, which he fails to supply where we most need it. In both cases, though, it is the rationality of the moral law that makes him think it must have the feature in question.

What does it mean to call it universal? Not just that it applies to all rational beings; also that it requires us to treat like cases alike. That seems reasonable, for it is part of our ordinary conception of morality. Perhaps exactly similar cases rarely occur, but it would be odd to hold that if two exactly similar cases did occur, what was right in the one could be wrong in the other.

What constitutes 'exact similarity'? Clearly, Kant thinks two situations can be exactly similar though they are different in time, and in place, and in the individuals concerned. But what other features can we abstract from? For Kant there is no real problem here. He is interested not in the action directly, but in the agent's maxim: the principle on which the agent acts. The agent, perhaps, needs money, and decides to borrow it, with no intention of paying it back. He may not consciously formulate any general principle, or maxim, but since we know his reason

31

for adopting this course, we can formulate his principle in general terms: 'Whenever I believe myself to be in need of money, I shall borrow money and promise to pay it back, even though I know this will never happen' (G 421). If that is his maxim, another action will be exactly similar in the relevant respects if its agent – whoever that may be – acts on the same maxim. And to will that it should become a universal law is to will that everyone should act on it.

Why should I act only on that maxim which I can at the same time will to become a universal law? Because if an action is right for me, it is right for everyone; and if it is not right for me, it is wrong. Kant's formulation is designed to help me identify certain actions as wrong. More exactly, it is the maxim that is shown to be wrong, but actions can always be described in different ways – as 'John's making a lying promise', or as 'that action which led to John's imprisonment' – and if we consider the action under the description given to it by the agent's maxim, then we can say that the action is wrong. (In this case, that would be 'John's borrowing money with a lying promise to pay it back, because he believes he needs money'.)

If an action is wrong, then abstaining from it must be obligatory; and if the *non*-performance of an action would be wrong – not the kind of thing one could will to become a universal law – the action must itself be obligatory. There will also be cases where it is possible to will a maxim as a universal law, but also possible to will its negation or various alternatives to it, equally universally. An example would be 'I shall always have porridge at breakfast'.

By categorical imperatives certain actions are *permitted* or *forbidden*, that is to say, morally possible or impossible, while some of them or their opposites are morally necessary, that is to say, obligatory. (M 221)

Where does duty come in? One acts out of duty only if one performs an obligatory action *because* it is obligatory, or abstains from one that is forbidden *because* it is forbidden. An action, or a maxim, which passes Kant's test is shown not to be wrong, but the question whether an action is right or wrong is the question whether it is *in accordance with* the law. As we have seen, one may perform an action that is obligatory, without one's action having any 'moral worth', because one did not act out of duty. If one does act out of duty, in fact, one's maxim changes: as Kant says, one 'incorporates the law into one's maxim', which now becomes something like 'I shall do whatever the law requires, which in this situation is XYZ'.

All of this is essential to understanding Kant's strategy; he explains none of it at the relevant point. Before going on to consider some examples, he reformulates the categorical imperative.

> Because the universality of the law by which effects take place constitutes what is properly called *nature* in the most general sense (as regards its form), that is to say the existence of things insofar as it is determined by universal law, the universal imperative of duty could also run: *act as if the maxim of your action were to become through your will a **universal law of nature*** (G 421)

So far we have seen a case for saying that, if a maxim is all right for me, it must be all right for anyone else. Kant now says, it must be all right if *everyone* else were to act on it together. This is not immediately obvious. Onora O'Neill points out that it would not be all right if everyone acted on the maxim 'I shall buy toy trains when I want, but I shall never sell any', for then there would be nobody to buy toy trains from.[7]

It is the new version that Kant wants to use as a practical test for maxims. He points out that it is a test people appeal to in ordinary life.

> In fact everyone judges actions by this rule, to see whether they are morally good or bad. Thus people say, 'If *everyone* allowed himself to deceive when he believed it to his advantage, or thought it proper to shorten his life as soon as he was thoroughly weary of it, or regarded the need of others with complete indifference, and if you yourself belonged to such an order of things, would you really be in it with the agreement of your will?' ... But such a law of nature is a *model* [*Typus*] for the assessment of maxims in accordance with moral principles. If the maxim of the action is not so constituted that it can stand the test in the form of a law of nature in general, it is morally impossible. Even the most ordinary understanding judges in this way; for the *law of nature* lies always at the basis of all its most everyday judgements, even judgements of experience. (P 69–70)

It is true that we often ask, 'What if everyone did that?' But it could be objected that the toy trains example shows it is the wrong question to ask.

The objection would be mistaken. If a maxim is all right for me, it must be all right for anyone else; and if it is all right for anyone else, it must equally be all right if everyone adopts it and acts on it together. Otherwise there would have to be some way of determining who could act on it and who could not. The toy trains example is misleading in this respect. What makes acceptable the policy of buying toy trains and never selling them is that the agent is well aware that other people are perfectly happy to sell them. If his maxim is 'I shall buy toy trains and not sell them, provided that others want to sell them', there is no difficulty.

Kant gives us four examples; the clearest is that of the lying promise. His objection is that the maxim cannot be right, because I cannot will that everyone should act in accordance with it.

> Thus I transform the demand of self-love into a universal law and frame the question in this way: how would things stand if my maxim became a universal law? Now I see at once that it could never hold as a universal law of nature and be consistent with itself; instead it must necessarily contradict itself. For the universality of a law which said that everyone who thought himself in need could promise what he liked, with the intention of not keeping his promise, would make promising itself impossible, and likewise the purpose of making the promise. For no one would believe he was being promised anything, but would laugh at all such utterances as idle pretence. (G 422)

He thinks there could not be a state of affairs in which everyone made lying promises whenever it suited them. The maxim 'cannot even be *conceived* as a universal law of nature without contradiction' (G 424). This is not quite right, though. There is no contradiction without an empirical assumption, that people will not go on trusting one another's promises, despite being always let down. Then we have a contradiction: people make promises, but there can be no such thing as promising. However, a similar argument would seem to rule out the maxim 'Let me always refuse bribes': if everyone always refused bribes, the practice of bribery could not exist. What is the difference?

With promising the contradiction really lies in the will, despite an assertion of Kant's to the contrary (G 424). I seek to exploit the practice of promising, and so I will that the practice should continue. Yet I also seek to will something inconsistent with that. With refusing bribes there is no such conflict. I do not will that the practice should continue.

Lying promises concern my relations with other people. As a parallel example where a maxim that concerns only myself gives rise to a similar contradiction, Kant gives us 'Out of self-love I make it my principle to shorten my life if its continuance threatens more trouble than it promises pleasure' (G 422). He says

> The only question remaining is whether this principle of self-love can become a universal law of nature. But one soon sees that a nature whose law it was to destroy life itself, by means of that same feeling whose function is to promote the furtherance of life, would contradict itself, and so could not exist as nature. Thus that maxim could not possibly hold as a universal law of nature, and consequently it is entirely opposed to the highest principle of all duty. (G 422)

He does not say there is any immediate conflict involved in deciding on suicide from the motive of self-love; as before, the conflict appears only when the maxim is taken to hold as a universal law. Again it depends on an empirical assumption, but one that is less obvious. It is that if people *always* killed themselves when things looked black, out of a desire to maximize their overall happiness in life, then that objective of theirs would actually be defeated. This is not implausible, though, since people often do take their future outlook to be far worse than it really is. Given that assumption, we have a conflict parallel to that in the lying promise example. I want to maximize my overall happiness; but I also seek to will something which, in its universal form, does not maximize happiness but reduces it.

This is not a general argument against suicide. Nor indeed is the other argument a general argument against lying promises. They both argue that a particular *maxim* must be wrong, on the grounds that if it were all right for me it would have to be all right for everyone, and that this leads to an incoherence. Kant did believe lying promises are always wrong, but it does not follow from what he says here. And he certainly did not think he had shown suicide is always wrong.

> Can one charge a great monarch who died not long ago with a criminal intention, because he carried a quick-acting poison with him, presumably in order that if he were captured in war, when leading his troops, he could not be forced to agree terms of ransom which could be harmful to the state? (M 423)

The monarch was Frederick the Great, whom Kant admired, and this appears in the *Metaphysics of Morals* as one of the many 'casuistical questions', questions not to be answered by a simple appeal to rules.

The third and fourth examples he considers in the *Groundwork* are importantly different from the first two. The maxims to be tested are 'I shall let my talents rust and devote my life solely to enjoyment' and 'I shall pay no attention to the needs of others'. In both cases Kant thinks there could be a society in which everyone did act on the maxim concerned, and he thinks the South Sea Islanders do let their talents rust. What is wrong with doing so is that the agent

> cannot possibly **will** that this should be a universal natural law or that it should be implanted in us as such through natural instinct. For as a rational being he necessarily wills that all the capacities in him should be developed, because they serve him, and are given him, for all sorts of possible purposes. (G 423)

Likewise with neglecting the needs of others:

> although it is possible that a universal law of nature could exist in accordance with that maxim, it is impossible to **will** that such a principle should hold everywhere as a natural law. For a will that decided in this way would conflict with itself, since many situations could arise in which one needed the love and sympathy of others, and in which, through such a law of nature sprung from one's own will, one would rob oneself of all hope of the assistance one wants for oneself. (G 423)

In both cases the objection is that it is impossible to *will* something. If by 'will' he meant 'want', as people sometimes think, he would be wrong both times. But Kant has a special conception of willing. To will is to want rationally. He does say this, earlier on in the second chapter, but very briefly, and with no indication of how important a point it is.

> Only a rational being has the capacity to act *in accordance with its idea* of laws, that is, in accordance with principles: in other words, it has a *will*. Since for the

> derivation of actions from laws *reason* is required, the
> will is nothing other than practical reason. (G 412)

Why must every rational being necessarily will that all its capacities be developed? Why must every rational being necessarily will complex projects of a kind liable to need the co-operation of other people? Kant does not say here; he does not even make it adequately clear that there are certain things reason requires us to want. But we know what they are, from the *Metaphysics of Morals*: one's own perfection and the happiness of others. He would have avoided much misunderstanding if he had spelt that out at this point. One cannot promote one's perfection fully without developing all one's capacities; nor can one promote the happiness of others without their help and assistance.

By not explaining this in the *Groundwork* he makes it baffling how he can reformulate the categorical imperative in terms of treating people as ends in themselves, and declare it equivalent to the other formulations. 'So act that you treat humanity, both in your own person and in the person of every other human being, never merely as a means, but always at the same time as an end' (G 429). As we saw before, the *Groundwork* leaves it vague what is meant by 'treating people as ends', though he gives us some idea by taking us through the four examples again and showing how, in each case, the maxims involved would treat people as means.

He reformulates the categorical imperative twice more, to introduce two further ideas, those of autonomy and of a kingdom of ends. These add relatively little.

The principle of autonomy is called 'the supreme principle of morality'.

> Autonomy of the will is the property of the will by which it is a law to itself (independently of every property of the objects of volition). The principle of autonomy is therefore: never to choose except in such a way that the maxims of one's choice are at the same time included as universal law in the same volition. (G 440)

Because the will is rational, it is a law to itself just to the extent to which the agent's choices conform to the requirements of reason alone – pure practical reason – and hence to the categorical imperative. One can also make choices that are rational only in a dependent way, as the means of achieving some end that one happens to want. Here the rationality is only the rationality of a hypothetical imperative.

> If the will seeks the law that should determine it *anywhere else* than in the appropriateness of its maxims for its own universal lawgiving, and therefore if it goes outside itself and seeks it in the property of any of its objects, *heteronomy* always results. Then the will does not give itself the law; instead the object gives the law to the will through its relation to the will. This relation, whether it depends on inclination or on representations of reason, allows only hypothetical imperatives to be possible. (G 441)

The will is now not a law to itself, since it does not provide itself with the end; instead, it gets it from elsewhere. So it is 'heteronomous', not autonomous.

When the will is autonomous it can be seen as giving the law to itself, because in willing the categorical imperative it is purely rational and not dependent on any desire or inclination external to reason. Hence, Kant says, the idea of autonomy is 'the idea *of the will of every rational being as a universally lawgiving will*' (G 431). This does *not* mean that the moral law is arbitrarily invented. It is no more arbitrarily invented than the laws of logic are. But like the laws of logic it is prescriptive and it is laid down by reason, on grounds that are purely rational and make no appeal to anything that is not rational. So far as I am autonomous, I legislate for myself exactly the same moral law that every other autonomous rational being legislates for itself. The metaphor of legislation implies prescriptivity, not that there is any place for arbitrariness.

Rational beings are ends in themselves. If they all acted rationally, in accordance with the moral law, they would constitute an ideally harmonious society in which everyone was governed by that law; a 'kingdom of ends'.

> I understand by a *kingdom* the systematic union of different rational beings through common laws. Now laws determine ends in accordance with their universal validity. Therefore if one abstracts from the personal differences between rational beings, and likewise from all the content of their private ends, it must be possible to conceive of a totality of all ends (both those of rational beings as ends in themselves and also the individual ends which each rational being must set for itself) in systematic interconnection – that is to say, a kingdom of ends, which is possible by the above principles. (G 433)

Here everyone can have their own individual ends, their own 'projects', because the moral law permits us to have such ends, though only insofar as they do not interfere with others, as we saw before. Such a kingdom of ends is possible, though not of course actual; 'yet this law remains in its full force, because it commands categorically: act in accordance with the maxims of a universally lawgiving member of a merely possible kingdom of ends' (G 439).

This final version of the categorical imperative is really just a more romantic way of expressing it; or as he elsewhere suggests, more mystical.

> I entitle the world as it would be if it were in accordance with all moral laws – as indeed it *can* be, given the *freedom* of rational beings, and as it *should* be, given the necessary laws of morality – a **moral world** … The idea of a moral world thus has objective reality … when it is taken as applying to the sensible world, but the sensible world construed as an object of pure reason in its practical use, that is, as a 'mystical body' of the rational beings in it, insofar as the free will of each of them under moral laws stands in thoroughgoing systematic unity both with itself, and with the freedom of every other. (A 808/B 836)

A PHANTOM OF THE BRAIN?

At the end of the second chapter of the *Groundwork* Kant says:

> By developing the concept of morality that is universally current, we have only shown that autonomy of the will is unavoidably connected with it or rather lies at its foundation. So anyone who takes morality to be something real, and not a chimerical idea lacking truth, must admit the principle of morality that has been brought forward. This chapter, therefore, like the first, has been merely analytic. That morality is not a phantom of the brain will follow if the categorical imperative, and with it the autonomy of the will, is true and absolutely necessary as an *a priori* principle. But this can be shown only by a *possible synthetic use of pure practical reason*; and we cannot venture on that without first providing a *critique* of this rational capacity itself. In the last chapter we must sketch enough of the key features of this critique to meet our purpose. (G 445)

Autonomy is fundamental, because the idea of autonomy is that of a rational imperative willed on purely rational grounds. But is morality more than an illusion?

The third and final chapter equates autonomy with freedom of the will:

> for what indeed can freedom of the will be except autonomy, that is, the will's property of being a law to itself? But the proposition 'The will is in all its actions a

law to itself' indicates only the principle of acting on no other maxim than one which can have as its object itself as a universal law. This however is just the formula of the categorical imperative and the principle of morality. So a free will and a will under moral laws are the same thing. (G 446-7)

Kant's main concern is to defend the thesis that the will is free; for without free will, moral action would not be possible, and there would be no place for moral responsibility. But he is wrong to *equate* free will with autonomy, and he does not do this elsewhere. The freedom that grounds moral responsibility must make it possible for us to make wrong choices as well as right ones. As he says in a note, 'Freedom is the greatest good and the greatest evil' (Rf 7217). So Kant should say that autonomy requires free will, but is not identical with it.

In later writings he makes things clearer by distinguishing between *Wille* and *Willkür*. Both words can be translated 'will', but a free *Willkür* is a will that is free in the ordinary sense, capable of choosing between the demands of morality and the demands of our non-moral ('pathological') motives and desires. We all have free *Willkür*, even the most wicked of us. 'To satisfy the categorical demand of morality is in the power of everyone at all times' (P 36-7). *Wille*, however, is the will considered as purely rational, and a free *Wille* is an autonomous will. Freedom of *Wille*, then, requires freedom of *Willkür*, but is not the same thing.

The freedom of will (*Willkür*) that Kant defends is incompatible with causal determinism – the thesis that whatever happens has some cause sufficient to bring it about. When people act freely their wills cause things to

44

happen, but nothing causes them to choose as they do.

> The *will* is a kind of causality that living beings have so far as they are rational, and *freedom* would be that property of this causality which allows it to be effective independently of outside *determining* causes. *Natural necessity* is the property of the causality of all creatures lacking reason, by which they are determined to activity through the influence of outside causes. (G 446)

He is contemptuous of those who try to reconcile free will and determinism by saying that we can be called free whenever we make choices that are unconstrained, though causally explicable.

> If I say of a man who has committed a theft that, by the natural laws of causality, this act was a necessary result of earlier determining conditions, so that it was impossible that it should not have happened; how can a judgement in accordance with the moral law make an alteration in this? How can we suppose that the act could have been refrained from, because the law says it ought to have been refrained from? In other words, how can that man be called entirely free at the time of acting and in relation to the action, if at the same time and in relation to the same action he stands under an unavoidable natural necessity? Some people seek a way out by suggesting that the *kind* of conditions that determine his causality by natural laws fit with a *comparative* concept of freedom. According to this, the term 'free effect' is sometimes applied to something whose determining natural conditions are *internal* to the being that produces the effect. An example is the action of a projectile when it is in free motion; here one uses the

word 'freedom' because while it is in flight it is not impelled from outside. Again, we call the movement of a clock a free movement, because it drives the hands itself, and the hands do not have to be pushed from outside. Similarly the actions of people are (on this view) still called free, even though they are also necessary as a result of their earlier determining conditions, because these actions are caused internally in accordance with our choice, by thoughts which our own powers bring up and by desires produced in us by circumstances which cause them. But this is a wretched subterfuge, by which some people still allow themselves to defer the issue, and think that by a little fiddling with words they have solved that difficult problem on the solution of which thousands of years have worked in vain, and which therefore can hardly be found so completely on the surface. (P 95–6)

If freedom were no more than this, 'it would be fundamentally no better than the freedom of a turnspit, which also moves by itself once it has been wound up' (P 97).

The behaviour of animals may be determined mechanically by whichever of their inclinations is strongest, but as rational beings we can choose which of our inclinations to follow, and whether or not to obey the moral law. Free *Willkür* in the proper sense is an inalienable property of rational beings; every choice that can be assessed morally arises from it.

If one seeks for its rational origin, every bad action must be regarded as though the agent had fallen into it directly from the state of innocence. For whatever his previous conduct may have been, and whatever the natural causes may have been that influenced him, and regardless of whether these causes are to be found within him or outside him, nevertheless his action is free and not determined by any of these causes. So it can and must always be judged as an *original* use of his will [*Willkür*]. He should have refrained from that action, whatever his temporal circumstances and relations may have been. For through no cause in the world can he cease to be a freely acting being. (R 41)

Many people nowadays would think that someone's action can be excused if we can find causes to explain it, but Kant firmly disagrees, and believes he is supported by popular opinion.

There are cases in which people show themselves so wicked from childhood on, despite an upbringing that produced good results with others, and so develop in wickedness as they progress into adulthood, that they are thought to be born villains, and quite incapable of improvement in their way of thinking about things. All the same they are judged for what they do and fail to do, and they are held guilty for their crimes; and they themselves (the children) find this as fully justified as if they remained as responsible as anybody else, despite the hopeless natural cast of mind ascribed to them. This could not happen unless we assumed that everything that springs from someone's will [*Willkür*] – as without doubt every intentional action does – has as its basis a free causality, which from early youth expresses the character of that will in its appearances (the actions). Because of the uniformity of the person's conduct these actions enable us to recognize a natural connection, but they do not make necessary the evil nature of the will, which is instead the consequence of the wicked and unchangeable principles that have been freely adopted, and which make him all the more reprehensible and worthy of punishment (P 99–100)

This may be going too far. But he has a strong case for saying that actions out of respect for the moral law would not be possible if we were just part of a deterministic system. A system of deterministic causes, operating on us, could bring it about that we acted in accordance with the law (and therefore rightly), but not that we acted out of respect for the law (so that our actions could have moral worth). To act out of respect for the law one must be influenced by the law itself. But the law is not part of the empirical causal order. For that reason he calls the freedom it requires 'transcendental'; it

must be thought of as independence from everything empirical and thus from nature in general ... Without that freedom (in this proper sense of the word), which alone is practical *a priori*, no moral law is possible, nor any moral assessment. (P 97)

To the question *why* someone chooses to adopt the moral maxim, or some alternative, there is nothing more to be said than that the choice is up to them, tempting though it may be to try to push the question further.

Neither the subjective ground nor the cause of this adoption can be known, although it is unavoidable to ask about it; for otherwise another maxim would be needed, into which this disposition was incorporated, and this other maxim would again have to have a ground. (R 25)

However, there is a difficulty in all this for Kant himself.

In the *Critique of Pure Reason* he had reached the conclusion that causal determinism must actually be true of the ordinary world of people and things in space and time. How can that be reconciled with the requirements of free will?

The *Critique* argued that the ordinary, empirically know-able world – also called the sensible world or the world of appearances (phenomena) – is 'transcendentally ideal'. It is the world *as we can know it*, but our knowledge of it is made possible by a set of concepts and by a spatio-temporal arrangement of things, both of which are in some sense due to us and to our mental capacities. This sensible world can be contrasted with the world 'as it is in itself', independ-ently of those conditions that make it knowable for us. This world as it is in itself Kant calls the intelligible world, or the world of *noumena*, for he thinks it is the world as it would be known to a pure intellect like God's; but of this intelligible world, and the 'things in themselves' that constitute it, we can strictly know nothing, though practi-cal reason may license certain assumptions about it. This, Kant thinks, makes it possible to find a place for free will.

> There is still a way out, namely to enquire whether when we think of ourselves through freedom, as causes acting *a priori*, we are not taking up a different standpoint from the one we adopt when we think of ourselves and our actions as effects that we can see before our eyes. (G 450)

To view ourselves as part of the sensible world is to see ourselves and all our actions as causally determined. But

> a rational being must regard itself *as intelligence* (and thus not from the side of its lower powers) not as

belonging to the sensible world, but rather to the intelligible world. It therefore has two standpoints from which it can consider itself and from which it can know laws governing the use of its powers and thus of all its actions. *First*, so far as it belongs to the sensible world, it can consider itself under natural laws (heteronomy). *Secondly*, so far as it belongs to the intelligible world, it can consider itself under laws which are independent of nature, and not empirical, but founded only in reason.

As a rational being, and so as belonging to the intelligible world, man can never think of the causality of his own will except under the idea of freedom. For independence from the sensible world's determining causes (which is what reason must always attribute to itself) is freedom. (G 452)

Because Kant thinks of free choice as really noumenal, and so as lying beyond the world we can know about, he says we can never explain it. 'Reason would overstep all its limits if it undertook to *explain how* pure reason can be practical, which would be exactly the same as the task of explaining *how freedom is possible*' (G 458–9).

But if we consider a particular choice, made at a particular time, the question remains: is it free or not? It cannot be both. To say that it is free is to say that antecedent conditions do *not* determine the choice; if it is not free, it is because they *do*. The two standpoints may be unavoidable for us, but they cannot both give us the truth. Though this does not come out in the *Groundwork*, it appears Kant really thinks that the particular temporal choice is always determined. What is free is an atemporal choice, for time is a feature only of the sensible world, and the intelligible world is outside time.

Pure reason, as a purely intelligible capacity, is not subject to the form of time, and is therefore not subject to the conditions of the temporal series. In producing an effect the causality of reason in its intelligible character *does not arise* or begin at a certain time. Otherwise it would itself be subject to the law of nature that governs appearances, insofar as this determines causal series in time, and its causality would therefore be nature and not freedom ... For the condition which lies in reason is not sensible, and so does not itself begin to be. (A 551–2/B 579–80)

Now in order to remove the apparent contradiction between freedom and the mechanism of nature in one and the same action ... one must remember what was said in the *Critique of Pure Reason* or what follows from it: that natural necessity, which cannot coexist with the freedom of the subject, applies only to those features of a thing that stand under conditions of temporality, and consequently only to those features of the acting subject that belong to him as appearance [i.e. in the sensible world]. To this extent the determining grounds for each of his actions lie in things that are past and *no longer in his power*, and amongst such determining grounds must be reckoned his past deeds and the character which in his own eyes, as phenomenon, is determinable by them. But the very same subject is on the other hand conscious of himself as a thing in itself, and considers his existence *so far as it does not stand under conditions of temporality*, regarding himself as determinable only through laws which he gives to himself through reason. In this existence of his there is nothing antecedent to the determination of his will. Instead every action, and in general every determination of his existence that changes in conformity with inner sense, even the whole series of states that constitutes his existence as a sensible being, is in the consciousness of his intelligible existence to be viewed as nothing but a consequence, never a determining ground of his causality as *noumenon*. (P 97–8)

Even if it makes sense to think of choice outside time, this will not yield what was wanted. We must now sharply separate free choice from any of the practical decisions we make in the course of our lives. There is no way for free choice to intervene in the temporal series, as our ordinary conception of moral responsibility requires. Kant never seems fully to appreciate how remote this atemporal freedom is from the common-sense conception of free will from which he started. No individual action can properly be free at all, since actions take place in time. Timeless free choice can only fix the entire empirical character that gives rise to the various temporal actions.

So considered, the rational being can now rightly say of every action he performs contrary to the law that he could have refrained from doing it, despite the fact that as appearance it is sufficiently determined in the past and is to this extent unavoidably necessary. For it, together with all the past that determines it, belongs to the single phenomenon of his character, which he provides for himself, and in accordance with which he ascribes to himself, as a cause that is independent of all sensibility, the causation of those appearances. (P 98)

This is implausible. It is one thing to say that every rational being must think of itself as free; quite another to say that every rational being must think of itself as making choices outside time.

The problem does not arise in any case for anyone who is not committed to holding that the thesis of causal determinism is true of the everyday world. Many people find determinism attractive, but often without much reason. And whatever problems there are in his conception of free will, Kant has given us a reason for taking very seriously the idea that the will *is* free in a sense not compatible with causal determinism.

Now I say that every being that cannot act except *under the idea of freedom* is, just for that reason, really free from a practical point of view; that is to say, all laws that are inseparably bound up with freedom are valid for him, just as if his will had been shown to be free in itself and on grounds valid for theoretical philosophy. I assert now that to every rational being that has a will we must lend the idea of freedom, under which alone he acts. For in such a being we think of a reason that is practical, in other words, a reason that has causality in respect of its objects. Now it is impossible to think of a reason which would consciously receive direction from elsewhere in respect of its judgements, since then the subject would ascribe the determination of his judging not to his reason, but to an impulsion. Reason must regard itself as the author of its principles, independently of outside influences; consequently as practical reason, or as the will of a rational being, it must be regarded by itself as free. That is to say, the will of a rational being can be a will of his own only under the idea of freedom, and from a practical point of view such a will must be ascribed to all rational beings. (G 448)

This is not very clearly put, but let us take first the theoretical rationality involved in judging. By saying that somebody judges or argues rationally one might mean either of two things. One might mean that he drew conclusions in accordance with principles that are, in fact, rational ones; this a computer does when it has been appropriately programmed. Alternatively one might mean that he argues rationally because he sees that this is how he ought to argue. In the latter case what he does cannot be fully explained in causally deterministic terms, because part of what explains the inference he makes is his recognition of the validity of rational principles. His recognition of these principles can be explained only by reference to the principles themselves, and they do not belong to any causal order – they are not the right kind of thing. So, *if* people can argue not only in accordance with such principles, but out of a recognition of their validity, a causally deterministic account of their behaviour cannot be adequate.

Likewise with practical reasoning. If people can act not just in accordance with the moral law, but out of respect for it, their awareness of that law must explain why they act as they do, and the moral law is not the kind of thing that can belong to the causal order.

But *do* people ever act out of respect for the moral law? Is it ever the case that a recognition of the demands of reason actually does influence our actions or our inferences? As Kant says, there is no prospect of using empirical means to establish the reality of pure practical reason.

> For something that needs to derive the proof of its reality from experience must depend on empirical principles for the grounds of its possibility; but by its very concept pure yet practical reason cannot possibly be held to be

dependent on experience in this way. (P 47)

Yet it is impossible for us to think of ourselves *except* as recognizing and responding to such rational requirements. In the theoretical sphere, to think of ourselves as not doing this would be to think of ourselves as judging and arguing along lines that may seem natural but have no claim to be reliable or valid. In the moral sphere it would be to think of ourselves as capable only of actions in accordance with the law, and never of actions performed out of respect for the law. It would be to think of ourselves as automata. Kant is reminded of the mechanical figures Vaucanson had made.

> Man would be a marionette or an automaton like Vaucanson's, constructed and wound up by the Supreme Master of all the Arts. Self-consciousness would indeed make him a thinking automaton, but his consciousness of his own spontaneity would be a mere delusion if it were taken for freedom. He could be called free only in the comparative sense [i.e. the sense in which 'freedom' can co-exist with determinism], in that the immediate determining causes of his movement, and a long series of their determining causes, are indeed internal to him. But the last and highest cause is to be found entirely in someone else's hand. (P 101)

It is an exaggeration to say that 'every being that cannot act except *under the idea of freedom* is, just for that reason, really free from a practical point of view' (G 448); but Kant's point is really that the argument has reached bedrock. We must think of ourselves as free, and there is no reason to think we are not free. No empirical evidence is relevant, since that can tell us only about what is empirically discoverable, which *a priori* laws are not. So nothing more can be said, or needs to be said. 'Here now is the extreme limit of all moral enquiry' (G 462).

In the *Critique of Practical Reason* he puts it a little differently. He now says that what is immediately given to us *a priori* is not an awareness of our freedom, but the moral law itself.

> Moreover the moral law is given, as it were, as a fact of pure reason, of which we are *a priori* conscious, and which is apodeictically certain, even if no example of its being precisely followed can be found in experience. Thus the objective reality of the moral law can be proved by no deduction, by no effort of reason whether theoretical, speculative, or empirically supported. So if we wanted to renounce its apodeictic certainty it could not be confirmed by any experience and thus proved *a posteriori*. Yet it stands firm in its own right. (P 47)

By a 'deduction' Kant means an argument that establishes something as justified.

The reason for the change is evident enough. In the *Groundwork* he equated freedom with autonomy, so that to think of oneself as free was the same as to think of oneself as bound by the moral law. He now sees that one might think of oneself as free without that: without recognizing the moral law, one might obey hypothetical imperatives and promote self-interested ends, thinking of oneself as free in doing so. Still, to claim that we just are conscious of the moral law, and that it is too fundamental to be derived from anything else, is distinctly plausible. We simply are conscious of the demands of morality; and this itself shows us that we are committed to the reality of freedom.

But something different and quite peculiar comes in the

place of this vainly sought deduction of the moral principle, namely that it serves conversely itself as a principle for the deduction of an unfathomable capacity which no experience can prove ... This is freedom. The moral law, which itself needs no justifying grounds, can prove not only the possibility but the actuality of freedom in beings who recognize this law as binding on them. (P 47)

Duty commands him unconditionally: he *ought to* remain true to his resolution. From this he *infers* correctly that he must *be able* to do it, and that his will is therefore free. (R 49n)

Many would agree with Kant that 'ought' implies 'can'. But what about those like Hume who think the 'ought' of an objective moral law is only a phantom of the brain? In a sense, they are not refuted. Freedom and the moral law may both be illusions; we have no *proof* that they are not. If they are, they are illusions we cannot get rid of. And equally there is no way of proving that they *are* illusions. If the idea of an autonomous will responding to a rational law is coherent – and we have seen reason to think it so – it cannot be shown that our wills are not of that kind. Proof and argument will get us no further than this. 'Nothing is left but *defence*, that is, to refute the objections of those who pretend to have seen more deeply into the essence of things, and on this ground brazenly declare freedom to be impossible' (G 459).

But given that we firmly believe ourselves able to respond to a rational moral law, is there much point in entertaining scepticism about it? Is it any more sensible than being sceptical about the objective validity of elementary logical laws? It is true that some distinguished philosophers have gone in for such scepticism, but that does not make it sensible. And it is not, after all, surprising that proof and argument should run out. We can prove that something is an *a priori* principle only if we have somewhere to start from, and in the practical sphere the only place to start from is the fact of pure reason – or, if we follow the *Groundwork*, the consciousness of freedom.

When Kant tells us that the moral law requires us to promote perfection and happiness, people have sometimes asked what his argument for this is, and sought to find arguments in his text. But it is now clear that here, as with the reality of the moral law itself, argument would be out of place. The moral law is simply given; and we recognize it as such.

> And thus we do not indeed comprehend the uncondi-
> tioned practical necessity of the moral imperative, but
> we do comprehend its *incomprehensibility*; which is all
> that can justifiably be asked of a philosophy that strives
> in its principles to the very limit of human reason. (G
> 463)

NOTES

1. D. Hume, *A Treatise of Human Nature*, II:3:3; ed. L. A. Selby-Bigge (Clarendon Press, Oxford, 1888), p. 415. (First published 1739.)

2. In his *Ethics: Inventing Right and Wrong* (Penguin, Harmondsworth, 1977), J. L. Mackie argues that our ordinary conception of morality is indeed mistaken.

3. Kant says that the distinction between analytic and synthetic methods has no direct connection with the distinction between analytic and synthetic truths (Pr 276n). Analytic truths are those that hold in virtue of nothing more than the laws of logic and the meanings of the terms involved. Synthetic truths are those that are not analytic.

4. See Mackie, *Ethics*, pp. 38–42, and J. McDowell, 'Aesthetic value, objectivity, and the fabric of the world', in E. Schaper (ed.), *Pleasure, Preference and Value* (Cambridge University Press, Cambridge, 1983), p. 4.

5 W. V. Quine, 'Natural kinds', in his *Ontological Relativity and Other Essays* (Columbia University Press, New York, 1969).

6. At least, that is a plausible reading of Hume's *Treatise*. But Kant could not have known about it, since the relevant parts had not been translated into German.

7. O. Nell (= O. O'Neill), *Acting on Principle* (Columbia University Press, New York, 1975), p. 76.

FURTHER READING

Introductory

H. B. Acton, *Kant's Moral Philosophy* (Macmillan, London, 1970).

J. Schneewind, 'Autonomy, obligation, and virtue: an overview of Kant's moral philosophy', in P. Guyer (ed.), *The Cambridge Companion to Kant* (Cambridge University Press, Cambridge, 1992).

R. B. Sullivan, *An Introduction to Kant's Ethics* (Cambridge University Press, Cambridge, 1994).

Less Introductory

H. E. Allison, *Kant's Theory of Freedom* (Cambridge University Press, Cambridge, 1990).

M. J. Gregor, *Laws of Freedom* (Blackwell, Oxford, 1960).

B. Herman, *The Practice of Moral Judgment* (Harvard University Press, Cambridge, Mass., 1993).

C. M. Korsgaard, *Creating the Kingdom of Ends* (Cambridge University Press, Cambridge, 1996).

O. Nell (= O. O'Neill), *Acting on Principle* (Columbia University Press, New York, 1975).

O. O'Neill, *Constructions of Reason* (Cambridge University Press, Cambridge, 1989).

R. B. Sullivan, *Immanuel Kant's Moral Theory* (Cambridge University Press, Cambridge, 1989).